Nat Love

History
Maker
Bios

Deborah Underwood

⌐ LERNER PUBLICATIONS COMPANY • MINNEAPOLIS

For Judith, Ian, Sarah, and Sophie

Publisher's note: Many of the dates that Nat Love gave in his autobiography are impossible to verify. The author and editor have used their best judgment in determining which dates to include in this text.

Lerner Publications Company
A division of Lerner Publishing Group, Inc.
241 First Avenue North
Minneapolis, MN 55401 U.S.A.

Website address: www.lernerbooks.com

Library of Congress Cataloging-in-Publication Data

Underwood, Deborah.
    Nat Love / by Deborah Underwood.
      p.   cm. — (History maker biographies)
    Includes bibliographical references and index.
      ISBN-13: 978–0–8225–7171–1 (lib. bdg. : alk. paper)
    1. Love, Nat, 1854–1921—Juvenile literature. 2. African American cowboys—
West (U.S.)—Biography—Juvenile literature. 3. Cowboys—West (U.S.)—
Biography—Juvenile literature. 4. West (U.S.)—Biography—Juvenile literature.
5. Pullman porters—United States—Biography—Juvenile literature. 6. Slaves—
Tennessee—Biography—Juvenile literature. I. Title.
    F594.L892U53 2008
    978'.02092—dc22 [B]   2007020772

Manufactured in the United States of America
1 2 3 4 5 6 – JR – 13 12 11 10 09 08

TABLE OF CONTENTS

INTRODUCTION

Thousands of African American cowboys rode the ranges of the Old West between 1865 and 1890. However, Nat Love was the only one who published a book about his adventures.

Western writers often stretched the truth to make their stories more exciting. Most of what we know about Nat comes from his own book. Sometimes it's hard to tell what is true and what is a tall tale. Even so, Nat's words give us a good picture of cowboy life in the Old West.

This is his story.

1 FINALLY FREE

Nat Love was born in a log cabin in Tennessee in June 1854. He never knew his exact birthday, because he was a slave. People didn't keep track of when slaves were born. Like many slaves, Nat was given the last name of his owner, Robert Love.

Nat's father was in charge of other slaves on the plantation. His mother helped in their master's kitchen and wove fabric for clothes. Nat had an older sister, Sally, and an older brother, Jordan. The family worked hard. They had little time to care for Nat.

The U.S. Civil War (1861–1865) began when Nat was six. Slavery was a major issue in the war. The South wanted to keep slaves. The North didn't want to allow slavery in the United States. When the North won in 1865, Robert Love didn't tell his slaves they were free. But the slaves finally found out and celebrated.

The generals of the Northern and Southern armies met at this house in 1865. They agreed to end the Civil War. Soon after, Nat and other slaves became free.

Even after they learned the news, some slaves kept working for their former masters. But Nat's father wanted to work for himself. He rented land from Robert Love in order to grow his own crops.

Times were hard for most former slaves. Nat's family had no money for food or clothes. They often ate ashcake, a flat kind of bread. Nat's mother made the ashcake by putting batter made from bran and water between two cabbage leaves. She cooked it under a pile of hot coals.

Nat's mother baked ashcake in the fireplace.

Nat and his family grew corn to eat.

Nat helped his father make brooms and mats from straw. His father sold them in town and used the money to buy seeds. Before long, corn and vegetables were growing in their field.

But then the family's life changed forever. Nat's father got sick and died. Soon after, Nat's sister and her husband died too. Their two daughters moved in with Nat, Jordan, and Nat's mother.

Nat's family, like these former slaves, still had to work hard after they were free.

Fifteen-year-old Nat had to take care of his family. While Jordan worked their land, Nat found a job at a neighbor's, six miles away. He was able to buy his family potatoes, bacon, and other food. He even bought his mother a beautiful red dress and bonnet. "She was more pleased with them than any queen [would have been] with her silks and satins," he wrote.

On Sundays, Nat visited a horse ranch near his house. The owner's sons paid Nat to break colts. Breaking a colt meant riding it until it got used to having someone on its back. It was a dangerous job. The boys would force a colt into a stall in the barn. Then Nat would climb onto its back. When the barn door was opened, the horse would jump around the farmyard trying to throw Nat off. Nat would hang on until the horse got tired. The boys paid Nat ten cents for every colt he broke.

Nat is breaking a horse in this drawing. It came from the book that Nat wrote about his life.

One day, the boys wanted Nat to break a horse named Black Highwayman. The horse was so big and wild that Nat said ten cents wasn't enough. He wanted fifty! They agreed on twenty-five cents. Nat tied the money in the corner of his shirt and got up on the horse. "Out of the barn we shot like a black cloud," Nat wrote, "around the yard we flew, then over the garden fence."

NAT'S LUCKY DAY

When a man raffled off a horse, Nat sold two chickens to buy a raffle ticket—and won! The man bought the horse back from Nat for fifty dollars. Nat wrote, "Mr. Johnson at once raffled him off again and again I won the horse, which I again sold for fifty dollars."[3]

This story could be true—or it could be one of Nat's tall tales!

Like this rodeo horse, Black Highwayman gave Nat a rough ride.

Nat clung on. They raced through fields and into a pasture where other horses were grazing. The horses fled, with Black Highwayman leading the rushing pack. Finally, the horse gave up and calmed down. But when Nat looked in his shirt for his money, he found that it had fallen out!

Nat liked riding horses and dreamed of seeing the world. He got his chance when his uncle came to live with them. With his uncle and brother around to run the farm, Nat was free to set out on his own.

2 HOME ON THE RANGE

Nat wrote that he headed west to Kansas in 1869, when he was about fifteen. Sometimes he hitched rides in farmers' wagons. Sometimes he walked. He ended up in Dodge City, Kansas, more than seven hundred miles from home. There he met the Duval outfit, a group of cowboys from Texas. He asked their boss for a job.

The boss told Nat he could have a job—if Nat could ride a horse called Good Eye. A cowboy saddled up Good Eye and put Nat on his back. This horse was wilder than any horse Nat had ridden. Good Eye bucked like crazy. But to everyone's surprise, Nat stayed on until the horse got tired.

The boss offered Nat a job for thirty dollars a month. He bought Nat a new saddle, spurs, chaps (leather leggings worn over pants), blankets, and a gun. Nat had everything he needed for his new career as a cowboy.

COWBOY CAPITAL

Dodge City, Kansas, was known as Queen of the Cowtowns. Its railroad tracks made it an important shipping center. Cowboys brought cattle to Dodge, where the animals were sent east on trains.

In the early days, the town had no police. Dodge City became known as a wild place—partly because of the cowboys who stayed there. After long weeks on the trail, they were ready to have fun.

Cowboy life wasn't easy. Many cowboys lived and worked in the wide, grassy plains of the central United States. On the trail, cowboys ate whatever wild animals they could shoot. They slept on blankets on the ground. Herds of running buffalo (bison) crushed anyone in their path. Storms poured huge hailstones from the sky. Thieves tried to steal the animals the cowboys protected. But Nat didn't complain. He wrote, "I gloried in the danger, and the wild and free life of the plains."

Running buffalo were a danger to cattle and cowboys. An adult male buffalo can weigh two thousand pounds and run forty miles per hour.

To keep cattle moving, cowboys rode behind and beside the herd.

One of the cowboys' jobs was delivering animals to ranches or to market towns where they would be sold. Sometimes the cowboys herded cattle and sometimes horses. Nat learned skills like roping and herding on these trips.

Roundups were another big part of Western life. Cattle grazed on the open plains. They could wander far from home and get mixed up with cattle from other ranches. The ranchers sent cowboys to sort the cattle by their brand, or ranchers' mark.

Dodge City, Kansas, in the 1870s

After about three years, Nat got a new job with the Pete Gallinger Company in Arizona. Nat became their chief brand reader. He went through cattle at roundups and picked out Gallinger's animals.

Nat still went on cattle drives too. Soon after he started his new job, Nat and thirty-nine other cowboys had to deliver a large herd of cattle to Dodge City. The trip went smoothly at first. But then, the cattle began stampeding (running wildly) almost every day. If something startled the herd, it would bolt. The cowboys had to chase the cattle to get them under control. Sometimes they got miles off course.

A stampede at night was even worse. One evening, the cowboys and cattle were caught in a severe storm. The frightened cattle stampeded. Nat wrote, "Imagine, my dear reader, riding your horse at the top of his speed through torrents of rain and hail . . . chasing an immense herd of maddened cattle which we could hear but could not see, except during the vivid flashes of lightning which [provided] our only light. It was the worst night's ride I ever experienced."

In a storm, lightning helped cowboys see their cattle. But lightning and thunder also frightened the herd.

By the time the cowboys had rounded up the herd the next day, they were thirty miles away from where they had started. As they traveled back to camp, the cowboys saw how dangerous their night had been. The ground was covered with holes and big rocks. Steep cliffs dropped off along the way. Nat was proud that they didn't lose a single animal during their wild night's ride.

Chasing cattle in the dark was dangerous. Nat and the other cowboys were riding through rocky country such as this.

3 THE COWBOY CONTEST

Nat's job took him all over the West. He claimed to know all the trails from Canada to Texas and from Missouri to the Pacific Ocean. The cowboys even traveled to Mexico to pick up animals. They met Mexican cowboys on those trips. Nat wrote that the Mexicans "knew a thing or two about the cattle business." He enjoyed trading tips with them.

AMERICA'S FIRST COWBOYS

The Mexican cowboys Nat met were called vaqueros. Vaqueros were working with cattle long before other cowboys arrived in the West.

Many cowboy tools and words came from the vaqueros. Cowboy hats are based on the vaqueros' wide-brimmed hats. The word *rodeo* comes from the Spanish *rodear*, which means "to surround." The term *buckaroo* comes from *vaquero*. (In Spanish, *v* sounds a lot like an English *b*, and *qu* sounds like *k*.)

Once, on the way home from Mexico, a group of Native Americans stopped the cowboys. They asked for an animal as payment for passing through their land. The cowboys refused—but they knew it might mean trouble later.

Some cowboys stayed awake to keep watch that night. The others slept with their boots on and their guns ready, just in case. When one of the guards gave the danger signal, the men leaped to their feet. A group of Native Americans began to scare the cattle so they would stampede.

The herd raced back and forth in the dark as the cowboys tried to control it. Bullets flew as the cowboys defended the animals. The Native Americans finally left, but the cattle kept acting strangely. Nat found out why the next morning. Many Native Americans had hidden in the tall grass around camp for the attack. The rushing cattle had trampled them to death. Nat said the victims were a horrible sight.

Native American warriors in the Southwest in the late 1800s

Their bad luck continued the next night. Nat was keeping watch. Around midnight, he heard a rumbling that grew louder and louder. A herd of stampeding buffalo was heading toward the cowboys.

The cowboys hopped on their horses and tried shooting the buffalo. Nat wrote, "[the buffalo] paid no more attention to us than they would have paid to a lot of boys with pea shooters." The stampede killed some of the cattle and trampled one of the cowboys.

Bison kick up a lot of dust as they run across the plains.

Deadwood, South Dakota, was a lively town in the late 1800s.

In the spring of 1876, Nat and the other cowboys took a herd of cattle from Arizona up to Deadwood, South Dakota. They reached Deadwood on July 3, ready to have some fun. The next day, they decided to have a roping contest with other cowboys in town.

Twelve cowboys entered the contest. The head cowboy picked out twelve wild mustangs (horses). Each cowboy had to rope his horse, put on a saddle, and climb on as quickly as he could. Nat wrote, "It seems to me that the horse chosen for me was the most vicious of the lot."

*Nat in his
Deadwood
contest clothes*

When the starting gunshot rang out, each cowboy raced to his horse. Nat got on his horse in exactly nine minutes. This was three and a half minutes faster than anyone else.

Next, the cowboys argued over who was the best at shooting. They held another contest that afternoon. Nat entered, along with a cowboy named Stormy Jim and several others who were famous for being good shots.

Each cowboy had to shoot at a target. He got fourteen shots with his rifle and twelve with his pistol. Nat wrote that he put all fourteen of his rifle shots in the bull's-eye. Stormy Jim, Nat's toughest competitor, got only eight. Nat missed two of the pistol shots—but Stormy Jim missed seven. Nat had won again!

Nat got a new nickname. "The name of Deadwood Dick was given to me by the people of Deadwood, South Dakota, July 4, 1876, after I had proven myself worthy to carry it," wrote Nat. "I have always carried the name with honor since that time."

4 CAPTURED!

During winter, the cowboys had
fewer jobs to do. But Nat still
managed to find excitement.

On October 4, 1876, Nat was searching
for stray cattle when he heard a war
whoop. A group of Native Americans was
riding toward him. Outnumbered, Nat fled.

As his horse galloped away, Nat fired shots at the attackers and they fired back. "Their bullets were singing around me rather lively," he wrote. One of the bullets shot right through Nat's leg and into his horse. The horse fell to the ground, dead. Nat kept shooting, using his horse's body as a shield. He kept fighting even after he ran out of bullets. He used his empty gun as a weapon until he passed out.

Like Nat, many Native Americans were skilled on horseback.

When he awoke, he was in the Native Americans' camp with his hands and feet bound. The Native Americans had put herbs on his wounds to help them heal. He learned he had killed five people during the battle. He wasn't proud of that fact. Nat wrote, "It is a terrible thing to kill a man no matter what the cause."

He guessed that the reason the Native Americans hadn't killed him was because he had fought bravely. Also, many of them were part African American. The group wanted Nat to stay with them and marry one of their women.

Some Native Americans lived in teepees on the plains.

In Nat's lifetime, many Native Americans welcomed former slaves into their communities. Some former slaves married Native Americans. Their sons, such as these men, served in the U.S. Army.

Nat pretended to go along with the idea. But he was really looking for a way to escape. He picked out a fast horse he could use to get away. He also took a strip of leather to use as a bridle. Nat hid it in his shirt. He could put the strip through the horse's mouth and hold onto the ends to guide the horse while riding.

After about one month, Nat's wounds were nearly healed. One night, Nat crept to where the horses were kept. He bridled the fast horse and leaped onto its back. He raced back to his home ranch in Texas. Nat said he rode one hundred miles in only twelve hours.

An African American cowboy pulls a stray longhorn out of the mud.

In the fall of 1877, Nat was on another hunt for stray cattle. He was a long way from the ranch when he got caught in a terrible storm. Rain and hail poured from the sky. Nat could barely see where he was going. Luckily, he came across a buffalo hunter's cabin. He spent the night there.

The next day, the hunter pointed Nat toward home. Nat rode until late that night, then made camp. He tied his horse's legs together so it couldn't run off. Then he settled down on the ground to sleep.

A strange squeal awoke Nat. He jumped up and grabbed his gun. His startled horse reared up on its hind legs. The rope holding the horse's legs together snapped, and the horse bolted. The sound of galloping hooves faded into the distance. Nat was alone on the plains.

Nat's saddle was heavy, but he didn't want to leave it behind. He put it on his shoulder and began to walk. Nat walked the whole night and the next day without food, carrying his heavy load. He killed a buffalo calf to eat, cutting off chunks of meat to carry with him.

A Western saddle weighs about forty pounds.

After Nat walked another day, he saw a blizzard approaching. He tried to walk through the storm, but he collapsed in the snow, exhausted. When he awoke, he was in camp with some of his cowboy friends. They had come looking for him. Nat wrote that when they found him, one of his hands was frozen onto his saddle. The other had frozen onto his rifle.

Nat's hands and feet were badly frozen. The cold had also damaged the skin on his nose and mouth so much that it came off. In a few weeks, Nat felt better. But he wrote, "I will never forget those few days I was lost and the marks of that storm I will carry with me always."

Blizzards in the West could bury fences and cattle. Nat was lucky to survive.

Nat Ropes a Cannon

Nat sometimes did crazy things. Once he tried to steal a cannon from a military fort! Nat raced his horse into the fort's yard, tossed his rope around the cannon, and pulled (BELOW). But the cannon wouldn't budge. Soldiers surrounded Nat. A law officer asked Nat why he had done it. Nat replied that he wanted to take the cannon home to fight the Native Americans. Amused, the man let him go.

5 NAT'S NEW JOB

By the late 1880s, the West was changing. The wide open plains were disappearing. Railroads stretched all over the country. Cattle no longer needed to be herded to faraway towns like Dodge City, where the trains ran. Ranchers could put cattle on trains in Texas instead. Rather than riding on dusty trails, people could take a train across the country in a matter of days. Cities and towns sprang up all over.

Nat didn't like the changes in the world around him. He decided it was time to leave his cowboy life behind. He went to Denver, Colorado. On August 22, 1889, he married a woman named Alice.

Although Nat's cowboy days were over, he still wanted to see the world. Nat applied for a job as a Pullman train car porter.

Nat (RIGHT) appears in this photo with his family.

Pullman train cars were the fanciest on the railroad. They had seats that changed into beds, letting people make long trips in comfort. Porters like Nat helped passengers with whatever they needed during their trips. Nat had to pay twenty-two dollars to have a special uniform made.

Nat's first trip went badly. Fussing over a train car full of riders was very different from herding cattle. "I suppose I made many blunders [mistakes] as the difference between a Pullman car and the back of a Texas mustang is very great," Nat wrote.

A Pullman palace sleeping car from the late 1800s

Porters kept Pullman cars, such as this Pullman passenger car, spotlessly clean.

One of his jobs was to shine passengers' shoes while they slept. He got the shoes mixed up and returned them to the wrong people. Nat wrote that the mix-up caused "a good sized rumpus" when the passengers awoke. People didn't give him tips. That made Nat mad. When he got back to Denver, he went back to the train office and quit.

Next, Nat sold groceries out of a wagon in Denver. Although business was good, he got restless after about a year. Then he tried the railroad again. The Pullman boss told him that to be successful, Nat needed to make the riders happy. Nat said that pleasing a few passengers was fine, but pleasing a whole carful was another matter!

Nat (FAR LEFT) stands with friends on his crew.

Nat in his porter uniform

Nat was much better at his job this time. He did anything his passengers needed. He got the morning paper for them and made up their beds at night. If riders were in bad moods, Nat tried to cheer them up. If they were sick, he took care of them. He began to get bigger tips and a higher salary. He started to enjoy the work more.

Riding rails may not have been as exciting as riding trails. But Nat still experienced moments of danger. Once, the train went off the rails in Colorado. It fell on its side in a ditch. Nat wrote, "We were forced to crawl out through the windows, like a prairie dog out of his hole."

FAIR PAY FOR PORTERS

During Nat's lifetime, there were few good job opportunities for African Americans. Many worked on farms or as household helpers. Train porters worked hard, but they were paid better wages and could work year-round.

Four years after Nat died, porters founded the first black labor union. The Brotherhood of Sleeping Car Porters worked for better salaries and working conditions. The union helped to get equal pay and treatment for blacks.

As a porter, Nat traveled the country from coast to coast. He saw San Francisco, California; Chicago, Illinois; and Boston, Massachusetts. He took great pride in the elegant Pullman cars. He also took pride in his country. He wondered why people visited Europe when there were so many beautiful things to see in the United States.

By the 1900s, Nat had many exciting stories to tell about his life. His friends encouraged him to write them down. So Nat wrote a book called *The Life and Adventures of Nat Love*. It was full of tales from his childhood, his wild cowboy years, and his travels as a train porter. It was published in 1907.

Nat died in Los Angeles in 1921. Since his childhood, he had gone from slavery to a life of travel and adventure. If even half of his stories are true, he led a remarkable life.

TIMELINE

NAT WAS BORN IN 1854.

In the year . . .

1865   Nat and the other slaves became free when the Civil War ended.

1869? he left home and got a job as a cowboy in Texas.
    Age 15

1872   he started a new job with the Pete Gallinger Company in Arizona.

1876   Nat won roping and shooting contests in Deadwood, South Dakota, and earned the name Deadwood Dick.
    Age 22

    he was captured by Native Americans.

1877   he roped a cannon at Fort Dodge, Kansas.
    he got lost in a blizzard.

1889   he quit his job as a cowboy.
    he married Alice.
    Age 35

1890   he got a job as a porter.

1905   he stopped working for the railroad.
    Age 51

1907   he published *The Life and Adventures of Nat Love.*

1921   he died in Los Angeles, California.
    Age 67

FACT OR FICTION?

Even experts don't know how much of Nat's book is true. However, common sense can tell us what *might* be true.

Nat said he rode one hundred miles in twelve hours. The Tevis Cup is a modern one-hundred-mile horse race. Very few people complete it in under twelve hours. But some do—so Nat's claim is possible.

Deadwood, South Dakota, published a weekly newspaper in 1876. That was when Nat said he won the title of Deadwood Dick. A contest should have been big news in a small town. But the newspaper did not even mention it. Some believe the contest is a legend.

But Nat's tales of cowboy life are like those that other cowboys wrote. Nat likely was, in fact, a good cowboy—and a good storyteller too.

Nat's one-hundred-mile ride might be a true story.

FURTHER READING

NONFICTION

Murdoch, David H. *Cowboy.* **New York: Alfred A. Knopf, 1993.** This book tells the history of cowboys and includes a section about vaqueros. It includes lots of photos of cowboy clothing and gear.

Savage, Jeff. *Cowboys and Cow Towns of the Wild West.* **Springfield, NJ: Enslow Publishers, 1995.** Historical photos from the trails help give a glimpse into the excitement and challenges of a cowboy's daily life.

Zemlicka, Shannon. *Quanah Parker.* **Minneapolis: Lerner Publications Company, 2004.** Read the story of a Native American warrior in Texas who lived at the same time as Nat. Quanah fought with cowboys like Nat to protect his people's land.

FICTION

Myers, Walter Dean. *The Journal of Joshua Loper, a Black Cowboy.* **New York: Scholastic, 1999.** This fictional diary of a teenage boy working on a cattle drive describes life on the trail.

WEBSITES

Diamond R Ranch (National Cowboy & Western Heritage Museum)
http://www.nationalcowboymuseum.org/diamondr/ index.html Follow the "Exhibits" link on this website to learn about cowboy gear, or click on "Printables" to find recipes for trail food.

The Life and Adventures of Nat Love
http://docsouth.unc.edu/neh/natlove/natlove.html Nat's entire book can be read online at this website. It includes more photographs of him and more drawings about his life.

Nevada Kids Page—Cowboy and Rodeo Glossary
http://dmla.clan.lib.nv.us/docs/kids/cr-glossary.htm Learn cowboy words and phrases, including words that came from the Mexican vaqueros.

SELECT BIBLIOGRAPHY

Allmendinger, Blake. *Ten Most Wanted*. New York: Routledge, 1998.

Durham, Philip, and Everett L. Jones. *The Negro Cowboys*. New York: Dodd, Mead and Company, 1965.

Katz, William Loren. *The Black West*. New York: Simon & Schuster, 1987.

Los Angeles Times. "'Deadwood Dick's' Book." October 22, 1906. 14.

Love, Nat. *The Life and Adventures of Nat Love*. Lincoln: University of Nebraska Press, 1995.

Seidman, Laurence Ivan. *Once in the Saddle: The Cowboy's Frontier 1866–1896*. New York: Alfred A. Knopf, 1973.

Slatta, Richard. *The Cowboy Encyclopedia*. Santa Barbara, CA: ABC-CLIO, 1994.

Tinkle, Lon, and Allen Maxwell, eds. *The Cowboy Reader*. New York: Longmans, Green and Co., 1959.

INDEX

Acknowledgments

For photographs and artwork: The images in this book are used with the permission of: © Bettmann/CORBIS, pp. 4, 13, 18, 39; Library of Congress, pp. 7 (LC-DIG-cwpb-03908), 10 (LC-USZ62-134227), 26 (LC-USZ62-46841), 29 (LC-USZ62-48370), 34 (LC-USZ62-100252); Images from Life and Adventures of Nat Love, Better Known in the Cattle Country as "Deadwood Dick" courtesy of The Rare Book, Manuscript and Special Collections Library, Duke University, Durham, North Carolina, pp. 8, 11, 16, 35, 37, 40, 41, 45; © Photodisc/Getty Images, p. 9; The Art Archive/Bill Manns, pp. 17, 33; © Royalty-Free/CORBIS, p. 19; © Jason Todd/Photonica/Getty Images, p. 20; Arizona Historical Society/Tucson, AHS #78153, p. 23; © Layne Kennedy/CORBIS, p. 24; © North Wind Picture Archives, pp. 25, 32; The Art Archive/National Archives Washington DC, p. 30; The Granger Collection, p. 31; The Art Archive/Culver Pictures, p. 38. Front cover: Library of Congress (LC-USZ62-46841). Back cover: © Photodisc/Getty Images.

For quoted material: pp. 10, 12 (top), 12 (bottom), 16, 19, 21, 24, 25, 27, 29, 30, 34, 38, 39, 42, Nat Love, The Life and Adventures of Nat Love (Lincoln, NB: University of Nebraska Press, 1995).